I Will Rise Above It!

*Who Invited the Spirit of Depression
to Dinner?*

Nadine Tyree Anderson

WestBow
PRESS
A DIVISION OF THOMAS NELSON

WestBow Press books may be ordered through booksellers or by contacting:

WestBow Press
A Division of Thomas Nelson
1663 Liberty Drive
Bloomington, IN 47403
www.westbowpress.com
1-(866) 928-1240

ISBN: 978-1-4908-0689-1 (sc)
ISBN: 978-1-4908-0691-4 (hc)
ISBN: 978-1-4908-0690-7 (e)

Library of Congress Control Number: 2013915820

Printed in the United States of America.

WestBow Press rev. date: 11/14/2013

Table of Contents

Dedication

This book is dedicated to my
parents, Bishop John Daniel Tyree, Sr.
and Bishop Lillian Ann Tyree, in their loving memory.

Mom and Dad, I feel your presence every day.
Because of you, my life has been blessed
with the richness of family and love.
I'm forever grateful to God
that He allowed me to be your daughter.

To my husband,
Reverend Warren T. Anderson.

Thank you for the way you love me and for the support
you have given me during this project.
I know it was God who brought us together.

To my son,
Tyrone Y. Jackson, Jr.

You are my joy and a gift from God.
I am so proud of you, and I believe with all my heart
that you are going to do great things through
Jesus Christ. I love you, son.
PS. Thank you for my hearts, my
granddaughters, Kyndall and Briya.

To my siblings,
Sheryl Tyree Hall,
John Daniel Tyree, Jr.,
Gayle Tyree Hall,
Lisa Mischelle Tyree.

*Thank you for your love
and for believing in everything I do.
I could not have accomplished this without your support.
Our bond is forever and for always.*

Acknowledgments

*I would like to give God all the honor and glory
for inspiring me to write this book.
He has allowed me to use my life's experiences
and the Word of God to enlighten His people.*

To the Church of Deliverance family:

*My love for the church goes without words.
I would like to say how much I love you and that
I could not have done this without your prayers
and support.*

Side Effects

Please note that reading this book may cause the following side effects:

- Some may sleep better.
- Some may find joy unspeakable.
- Some may be filled with glory.
- Some may be delivered.
- Some may feel uplifted.
- Some may be able to detect and disable the spirit of depression.
- Some may be able to help others.
- Some may know there is hope.
- Some may understand that they are not alone.
- Some may feel free.
- Some may be able to stop the voice of depression in its tracks.
- Some may laugh.
- Some may know they have a future.
- Some may know how important they are.

Introduction

I'm not really dealing with the world's depression, even though I believe this book will help. I am confronting the spirit of depression, which is an enemy of believers and one of the weapons the adversary, the devil, uses against God's people. This has nothing to do with how strong or weak you are in Christ. It has everything to do with the fact that this is war—spiritual warfare. It does not matter whether you are *saved* or how committed you are to God—a choir director, a revivalist, or a pastor of a church. This spirit lurks and seeks out the strongest of saints and thrives on the weakest.

I am writing this book to you, or to people you may know, who suffer from depression, to tell you that your feelings are very real and not crazy. The good news is that there is a way out of the spirit of depression. I call depression a spirit because it is not you. It is not who you are. Yes, it looks like you, moves like you, and speaks like you. This spirit takes over your body to control you. It is an intruder seeking whomever it can devour. The bottom line is, depression's ultimate goal is to talk you to death. Depression can be lethal; therefore you have to fight spirit with spirit. That means you must fight the spirit of depression with the

Holy Spirit and the Sword of the Spirit, which is the word of God! The Word says, "No weapon formed against me shall prosper" (Isaiah 54:17). Believe me depression is one of Satan's sneakiest weapons.

I know you do not know me, but I have had the opportunity to minister and conduct seminars on this needed topic. The responses have been overwhelming. It was a blessing to see that people were made aware of this spirit of depression, or even delivered from it. So now I wish to share this book with everyone so that others will be delivered and will learn how to fight this negative spirit.

Even though I am not a physician, I have written this book from my own personal experiences with depression and by the inspiration of God. This book is very important to me because it will help you to know the voice of depression and how to disable this spirit by using your weapons against it. You never know when the spirit of depression will visit, but you can be prepared through awareness of God's Word and the power of our Lord and Savior. It is my sincere hope that it will help you as much as it has helped other believers and me to *rise above it*! Praise God!

So be encouraged to know that God really cares and loves you. Please do not delay reading this book and see what God has inspired me to write. Also, please give a copy of this book to a friend or a loved one. You never know whose life you will save or change; it might be your very own.

You do not have to invite the spirit of depression to dinner; it will unexpectedly show up and in its hands will be nothing but turmoil and self-destruction. So, guess who's coming to dinner? Believe me, it's not Sidney Poitier (smile), because things do get better.

Yours because of Jesus Christ,
Reverend Nadine Tyree Anderson

CHAPTER 1

Who Invited the Spirit of Depression to Dinner?

The Spirit of DEPRESSION

Anxiety in a man's heart weighs it down, but a good word cheers it up
Proverbs 12:25

aNta design ☺

"So get ready for a good word!"

Yes, who did invite this spirit to dinner? The answer is no one. It never needs an invitation. It just shows up! If you've ever dealt with or you are now experiencing this spirit, you know what I mean.

Let us just imagine. It's a beautiful Sunday evening. Dinner is on the table, and you reluctantly come to the dining room table. The family is seated all around and everyone, but you, is smiling and laughing. You're so depressed that you almost dare someone to snap you out it. Sound familiar? Just keep reading. You stick out like a sore thumb. You're down, depressed, and defeated—a feeling you cannot explain or shake off, nor do you really know why it just came out of nowhere. Who is this person? This isn't you, and the reason why I know this is because someone at the dinner table may ask, "What's wrong, Joann? You're not acting like yourself."

You're not acting like yourself. That's because it's not you. I repeat, "It is not you!" It is the spirit of depression that now sits there and does a very good impression of you. It has come to do actually what the adversary has told it to do, and that is *to steal, kill, and destroy you!* This spirit truly comes to steal your hopes, rob you of your dreams and visions, and kill your spirit, body, and soul, if it can.

So now you say, "Nothing is wrong," and the family continues with dinner. The father asks John to pass the peas, and you say, "Why did you ask John to pass the peas? Is something wrong with the way I pass the peas? I'm not good enough? What's wrong with this family?" So now you storm out of the room to your bedroom, as if the world came crashing down and to you the world has done so. Remember, this isn't really about peas.

The spirit of depression wants to separate you from God and your loved ones and get you alone. So you now do the worst thing ever. You close the door to your room. You just closed out everyone and locked yourself in with the enemy.

Now it can talk to you. It reminds you of your past failures, past regrets, past hurts. It wants you to believe the accomplishments of your family and friends, but not yours. It tries to convince you that you have no purpose. It can be very convincing, but the devil is a liar! I like saying that! If that is not bad enough, this spirit says, "remember when your cat, Sadsack, died five years ago?" And you repeat it, "My cat died!" That's all you needed to push you over the edge. All it wants is one tear to fall down your cheek, just that one tear, and there it is, so now it's on. The floodgates are now open. You lose your face. You can't get words out because you can't breathe. You are crying very hard—you know, that type of cry when your stomach ends up in your back and your pillow is so wet that you turn it over because it has become so uncomfortable. Have you ever been there? Believe me if you live long enough, you will, and I hope this book will help you, when those times come, to recognize this spirit and get it before it gets you.

Remember this is spiritual warfare, and we must fight spirit with spirit, that is the spirit of God. The Bible says, "God is a Spirit; and they that worship Him must worship Him in spirit and in truth" (John 4:24).

So please know you're not alone. We must depend on the right resource—our heavenly Father. This is not your battle. Believe me, God is good at fighting this war.

When my son was about seven years old, he asked me to watch the WWF (wrestling) with him. This wasn't my cup of tea, but I thought this would be a good mom-and-son bonding moment. So I sat on the bed beside him and began to watch. I mean I really began to watch with interest. This is what I saw naturally and spiritually. It was a tag-team match. One of the team members was fighting in the ring and his teammate was on the outside of the ring, holding on to the ropes and repeatedly reaching out to him and saying, "Tag me, just tag me!" But he wouldn't tag his partner. His teammate tried and tried to get his attention, but he would not let his partner fight his battle. He would not let him in. Are you seeing where I'm going with this? Suddenly the wrestler who was winning got on top of the ropes. The beaten fighter just looked up and stood there as the other wrestler jumped on top of him and pinned him down. The referee stood over them and counted one, two, three, you're out! It was all over.

Jesus is saying, "You are not in this fight alone." He is on the outside of the ring with His hands reached out to you, waiting for you to tag Him. Just call on Him, and He will answer you in the time of trouble. This is what the Word says. So don't fight this battle on your own. It was never meant for you to do so. Jesus is just waiting for you to tag Him. Can you imagine the adversary thinking he is going to fight you alone and you immediately tag Jesus and He comes into the ring, ready to defend you? Yes, you! What a surprise to the enemy and a relief to you!

The Bible says, "The Lord your God which goeth before you, he shall fight for you, according to all that he did for you in Egypt before your eyes" (Deuteronomy 1:30).

Reflections

(Use this page to write your innermost feelings, prayers, or thoughts.)

Date:_____

Chosen Scripture:_____

_____

_____

_____

_____

_____

_____

_____

_____

_____

Reflections

(Use this page to write your innermost feelings, prayers, or thoughts.)

Date:_____

Chosen Scripture:_____

_____

_____

_____

_____

_____

_____

_____

_____

_____

Reflections

(Use this page to write your innermost feelings, prayers, or thoughts.)

Date:_____

Chosen Scripture:_____

_____

_____

_____

_____

_____

_____

_____

_____

_____

Reflections

(Use this page to write your innermost feelings, prayers, or thoughts.)

Date:_____

Chosen Scripture:_____

_____

_____

_____

_____

_____

_____

_____

_____

_____

Reflections

(Use this page to write your innermost feelings, prayers, or thoughts.)

Date:———————————————————

Chosen Scripture:————————————

———————————————————————

———————————————————————

———————————————————————

———————————————————————

———————————————————————

———————————————————————

———————————————————————

———————————————————————

———————————————————————

CHAPTER 2

The Spirit of Depression
Wants to Talk You to Death

There are seven things the spirit of depression wants you to do:

1. To doubt God
2. To denounce what God can do in your situation
3. To separate you from God
4. To isolate you from God and your loved ones
5. To take your God-given life and leave your family with unanswered questions
6. To never reach your intended purpose
7. To end your seed (naturally and spiritually)

To every positive word of God, the devil has a negative word. Let's use the scripture that says, "The joy of the Lord is my strength." The opposite of joy is sadness. The opposite of strength is weakness. So the devil knows that the prolonged sadness of God's people will bring forth weakness in mind, body, and soul. At least that's what he hopes. The devil is counting on your lack of faith and knowledge of God's Word. Hosea 4:6 says, "My people are destroyed for the lack of knowledge." See, it's all right for you to know that "weeping may endure for a night", but the devil doesn't want you to know the rest of the sentence, "but joy cometh in the morning", to depend on it. So he sent out the spirit of depression, and the spirit of depression does its job very well. Its objectives are to get you *to lose faith* in God, *not to trust* His word and finally, to *separate you* from the love of God. The devil's end result is *for you to end your God-given life*!

The spirit of depression serves no purpose unless you give it one. It has no regards for gender, race, age, status, socioeconomic class, or political affiliation. Depression is an equal opportunity spirit. It doesn't care if you're a white-collar or blue-collar worker, one who lives uptown or downtown, a bishop, a pastor, an evangelist getting ready to run a revival, or an usher at the church doors.

The spirit of depression is actually weak by itself and needs help in order to make its case. It wants you to believe that life is not worth living and there is no way out of your life's situations. It eventually wants to make you believe that death is your only solution. *Wrong!* The devil is a liar! I do like saying that! Why don't you give it a try. Yes, right now." Tell the devil he is a liar! Do this for you and your loved ones.

The spirit of depression needs someone who will give it an ear or two—in other words a one-person audience. This spirit would love to be your event planner to plan your evening with the atmosphere of darkness and invite its friends—doubt, hopelessness, mayhem, and self-pity. It wishes to set your table with confusion and sits down to entertain you with thoughts of defeat and uncertainty. Tell depression there will be no show tonight! Remember, "Don't feed it and don't eat what it tries to feed you." As a matter of fact, command it to leave the room and not return. This is the way the scripture instructs us to deal with this spirit, "Resist the devil and he will flee from you" (James 4:7).

Once again, the spirit of depression is a killer of your will, spirit, dreams, and hopes. It will even try to diminish your successes. It is a destroyer of purpose and life. It doesn't want you to see what tomorrow will bring. It places blinders on you so you can only see one way. It wants you to stay focused on the part of the Scripture that says, "weeping may endure for a night" and not on what comes after, which is this: "but joy cometh in the morning." It doesn't want you to know that there are options—a way to escape, a new beginning, or a totally new direction. Please remember that one day or one moment can completely change your entire life.

God can take you from right where you are and catapult you ahead of those who said you were not going to make it, those who looked down on you, those who have plotted against you, or those who think they are holding you back. Our God can catapult you up and over. He can take you beyond their thinking and place you in a better position, or take you to another level.

The Bible says, "For promotion cometh neither from the east, nor from the west, nor from the south. But God is the judge: He putteth down one, and setteth up another" (Psalm 75:6:7). Our God is a God of promotion.

The tough challenges you face can cause you to have moments in your life that you don't understand: feelings of being sick and tired of being sick and tired. You may feel that you're in this all alone and you're not going to make it, but you cannot—I repeat—you cannot remain in that state of mind. The spirit of depression wants to *talk you to death!*

The Vocabulary of the Spirit of Depression (Depression Has a Voice)

The spirit of depression does not want you to recognize its presence; its strength is catching you off guard. It wants to make you believe those negative thoughts and feelings are yours and yours alone. "The devil is a liar." Depression can dish it out, but cannot take it when you fight back and put it in its place. Put depression back in its pit with words of victory. My sisters and brothers, stand up against it and talk back to it. You may not be able to talk back to Mom or Dad, but you sure can talk back to depression. In this chapter I have listed the vocabulary of depression. Below are words it uses to try to defeat you. Read them so you will recognize its voice. Victory has a vocabulary too, and it is speaking loud and clear. The words of victory are listed as well, so you can repeat them as often as you need to override the voice of depression.

Vocabulary of Depression

1. Nobody loves you.
2. Nobody wants you.
3. You never will.
4. It will never change.
5. You're ugly.
6. It will always be like this.
7. You serve no purpose.
8. No one can help you.
9. Where's God now?
10. See, I told you.
11. Just end it … right now.
12. There's no hope.
13. Nobody understands.
14. Why me?
15. You're no good.
16. You live a faithful life but look what happens.
17. It will never happen.

18. You're not good enough.
19. You can't go on like this.
20. You're better off dead.
21. No one will miss you.
22. No one will look for you.
23. Look at you! Look at you!
24. There's no way out.
25. You're not happy.
26. No one will listen.
27. You're so slow.
28. Will you never learn?
29. You're stupid.
30. You're still single.
31. You won't amount to anything.
32. Why didn't you?
33. They could have.
34. They won't.
35. They should have.
36. You're broke again.
37. Remember when your cat died?
38. You're hopeless.
39. You're defeated.
40. You'll never get that job.
41. You're so fat.
42. Everybody gets ahead except for me.
43. I haven't accomplished anything.

Please feel free to add some of your own. I'm pretty sure you can think of more, so go ahead and list them. Get familiar with them, so you will recognize the voice when you hear it and can say, "Yeah, wait a minute, that's not me. It's the spirit of depression speaking," and begin speaking words of victory.

The Vocabulary of Victory
(Victory Has a Voice too!)

Vocabulary of Victory

1. I'm more that a conqueror.
2. God loves me.
3. I can do all things through Jesus Christ, who strengthens me.
4. There is nothing too hard for God.
5. The Lord is my shepherd. I shall not want.
6. I am highly favored.
7. Fear not. The Lord will help thee.
8. I will make it. I can make it.
9. I am not alone.
10. You can't have my smile.
11. Count it all joy. In all things give thanks.
12. Thou art with me.
13. I am fearfully and wonderfully made.
14. Weeping may endure for a night, but joy comes in the morning.

15. I can do this.
16. With God all things are possible.
17. Jesus said, "I will see you again, and you will rejoice, and no one will take away your joy."
18. Put your hope in God.
19. I trust God. I trust God.
20. Depression, you have no authority.
21. I'm delivered by the power of Jesus Christ.
22. I'm free.
23. Lord, I give this to you.
24. Lord, I commend this to you.
25. The joy of the Lord is my strength.
26. All things work together for good to them that love God.
27. I won't give up.
28. Lord, I give it to you.
29. I release this to God.
30. I want to live. I will live.
31. Hallelujah! Hallelujah! Hallelujah! (Reader, go off into praise.)
32. Spirit of depression, I recognize you, and you are not welcome here!
33. I will rise above it!
34. The Lord will never leave me nor forsake me.
35. Lo, I am with you always.
36. I will see you through this.
37. Hold on.
38. I, your God, love you.

39. I'm stronger than this.
40. I am strong. I am strong.
41. I'm not defeated.
42. Today is a good day.
43. Today is a good day to live.
44. Thank You, Lord. Thank You. Thank You. Thank You. Thank You.

(Note: Giving the Lord praises of thanks is a major weapon against depression.)

I'm pretty sure you can think of some more, so go ahead and list them. Remember the spirit of depression is created to bring you to an empty place. It does not want you to be prepared. Again its strength is to catch you off guard and make you believe you're in this alone. But thanks to God, you're not! As a soldier prepares for war, so must we prepare and be ready for these battles.

Reflections

(Use this page to write your innermost feelings, prayers, or thoughts.)

Date:_____

Chosen Scripture:_____

_____

_____

_____

_____

_____

_____

_____

_____

_____

Reflections

(Use this page to write your innermost feelings, prayers, or thoughts.)

Date:_____

Chosen Scripture:_____

_____

_____

_____

_____

_____

_____

_____

_____

_____

Reflections

(Use this page to write your innermost feelings, prayers, or thoughts.)

Date:_____

Chosen Scripture:_____

_____

_____

_____

_____

_____

_____

_____

_____

_____

Reflections

(Use this page to write your innermost feelings, prayers, or thoughts.)

Date:_____

Chosen Scripture:_____

_____

_____

_____

_____

_____

_____

_____

_____

_____

Reflections

(Use this page to write your innermost feelings, prayers, or thoughts.)

Date:_____

Chosen Scripture:_____

_____

_____

_____

_____

_____

_____

_____

_____

_____

CHAPTER 3

I Will Rise above It

It is so important for believers to know it's all right to cry and not only cry, but go ahead and kick, scream, and shout. Give yourself permission to express your true feelings. God wants you to be honest with your thoughts and emotions. God already knows, so tell Him. Remember on the Mount of Olives Jesus prayed, "O Father, if it be possible, let this cup pass from me: *nevertheless* not as I will, but as thy wilt" (Matthew 26:39). See, we must tell God how we feel, but don't forget to say, '*nevertheless* God'. Your conversation should be something like the following: God, I have been going through this situation for some time and I really don't think you're with me at all, but 'nevertheless' I am going to trust you. I know you're God. I know you said in your word, "You'll never leave me nor forsake me." Allow yourself ten to fifteen minutes to get it all out, then say, '*nevertheless* God' for who He is and what you know He can do and has done for you.

Remember your testimonies and triumphs of the past and tell the spirit of depression what God has done for you time after time and what you believe He will do again. Believe me … it works!

Make a list of all your accomplishments—big or small. Make another list of all the people you have touched. This one can be a little tricky, because if you have touched ten people in your life, there are fifty more people you are not even aware of. These are some tools that will allow you to see your true value to God and others. Keep reading as I have more tools in later chapters.

You see, problems are just situations magnified. Think about it. We live in a world today where people are looking at believers—how they carry themselves, handle crises, disappointments, problems and troubles. Let's say, if something unfair happens to you on your job, I guarantee co-workers will be watching how you handle the situation—whether you're going to tell somebody off, or take a stand and say, 'Lord, I give this matter to you' and walk away with your head held high. You don't have to be a super hero, but you must have more than a conquering attitude and trust God's Word.

Our Christian lifestyle through the Word says we have hope—the belief that there is nothing too hard for God. We must say that we are committed and will let nothing separate us from the love of God.

So as a Christian, am I saying we don't have problems—heartaches, mishaps, sickness, hurts, death, grief, misunderstandings, confusion, financial concerns, doubts, children who have gone astray, broken relationships, broken hearts, and feelings of loneliness? Oh, no! But what I am saying is this: "The Lord is my shepherd; I shall not want" (Psalm 23:1); "If you ask anything in My name, I will do it" (John 14:14); "He shall deliver thee from the snare of the fowler" (Psalm 91:3); "And we know all things work together for good to them who love God according to his purpose" (Romans 8:28); "I will never leave you nor forsake you" (Hebrews 13:5).

So if God's Word is true—and it is—today you don't have a problem, but what you have is a situation and Jesus will see you through it. You shall *rise above it!* In other words, we all are going through things in life. Jesus, our Savior, is our problem-solver; so where is the problem? Remember it's just a situation. I'm not saying we should be in denial. However, something only becomes a problem when we allow the situation to overwhelm us, or when we lose our faith in what we know to be true, and that is with God all things are possible, if we believe. "With men this is impossible; but with God all things are possible" (Matthew 19:26).

Have you ever had a 'God-are-you-up-there moment?' Well, I have, and let me tell you what God showed me. I lived in Washington, DC. The city was being bombarded with snow. The weather person said, "Get your shovels ready; this is a winter storm advisory for a couple of days." Well, I really didn't pay much attention. However, eight inches of snow came that night, and I said, 'Never again will I not be ready.'

So again the weather person said, "It is going to snow approximately twenty inches." Well, I was in the grocery store with my shopping cart, picking up many essentials. This snowy weather went on for a couple of days, and I noticed every time I went to the store and stepped on the mat to enter, the doors would automatically open. Even though no one was there, it just opened to the store that awaited me. Somehow the doors worked with no one visibly there. I didn't see anyone, but the doors opened by themselves. Just because we don't see God, that doesn't mean He is not working on our behalf, and I want you to know He is opening that door to your storehouse. Our government may threaten to close down, but remember that heaven is always open and that God is still on the throne at work for you! Trust God. This is something we have to have in our spirit: I trust God—I trust God! Trust is like a key that unlocks the chamber to everything that God offers and will give to His believers.

Picture this (no pun intended): The devil takes your situation to his dark room. He begins to develop it, to enlarge it, yes, to blow the situation up to a 3x7 or 8x10 or even 11x14 or to whatever size it takes to make you feel the situation is just hopeless—like you're drowning and going down for the last time—to get you to believe it's beyond God's control.

The Bible says, "When thou pass through the water, I will be with thee; and through the rivers, they shall not overflow thee; when thou walkest through the fire, thou shalt not be burned; neither shall the flame kindle upon thee" (Isaiah 43:2).

I remember when I was learning how to tread water in our community pool. I repeatedly told my instructor who was within arm's reach in the water that I was drowning. I can't remember how many times I stated this, but he replied, "Nadine, as long as you're talking, you're breathing; and as long as you're breathing, you're not drowning.' Guess what? *You're not drowning.* The devil is a liar! You are still breathing.

So when you feel like you're drowning, you're not. Depend on God's Word. He will hold you up with His right hand. The Bible says, "For I, the Lord thy God, will hold thy right hand, saying unto thee, fear not; I will help thee" (Isaiah 41:13). Who is better to hold your head above water than God himself?

My friends, take this moment to relax and breathe. Go ahead and inhale the name of Jesus and now exhale the name of Jesus. Repeat this exercise again. You are treading, you are still alive, and God has given you another day, another opportunity to walk in your greatness, to marvel at how fearfully and wonderfully He has made you. God does not make any mistakes. We may not always understand God, but the Bible says, "For my thoughts are not your thoughts, neither are your ways my ways, saith the Lord" (Isaiah 55:8).

So stop trying to figure God out because you cannot. Just love Him, trust Him, and read His Word to know Him better. Ask God to open up the Word to you and to give you understanding, or place someone in your life who can guide and direct you. Give God the opportunity to change things, to bring down those strongholds, to give you a new day, and to make your crooked road straight.

In the Olympics there are runners who jump hurdles. The objective is to jump over them and not to go around or go under or knock them down, but to *rise above them*. The runners look at the situation, size it up, and then rise above the obstacles that stand in their way, the barriers that keep them from their blessings, and the walls that separate them from their purposes, goals, and desires. The runners never look back, but keep their eyes looking straight ahead.

When you rise above the opposition, you place that situation, problem, crisis, worry, and concern behind you, and this will cause you to move forward in God. In other words, this can elevate you to a higher place in God. The Word says, "Delight thyself also in the Lord and he will give thee the desires of thine heart" (Psalm 37:4). Notice the words, "he will give." That's God! He will give you the right desire of your heart, and that desire will line up with His desire for you.

I boarded a fight to Jamaica and the ride was very smooth. Then all of a sudden the plane began to shake, rattle, and roll from side to side. The pilot announced, "Sorry, we've entered into some rough weather and are experiencing turbulence. But don't worry. We are going to elevate over the situation to *rise above it*." When you allow God to raise you above the situation, you will be placed at a higher level in Him. Yes, a higher level. So hold on and don't give up. Remember what you're experiencing now, will take you to a higher place.

The story of Zacchaeus found in Luke19:1-10 will help me demonstrate how you can rise above your life's situations. The Bible says that Jesus was going through Jericho. Zacchaeus, who was a rich tax collector, wanted to see Jesus. The scripture also says that Zacchaeus was short in stature. Now of all the things the Bible could have mentioned, it placed emphasis on Zacchaeus' height. So if you don't mind me using my imagination, let's say that Zacchaeus was about four-foot-eight. The Bible says, "He sought to see Jesus." In order to *rise above it*, you have to seek the right things. You cannot look to man, money, or even material things to bring you to a place that only Jesus can bring you out.

Zacchaeus ran down toward the crowd of people who all wanted to see Jesus. The Bible says, "Because of the press, he could not see Jesus." There stood in front of him a five-foot-four problem. As Zacchaeus looked around he saw problems of every size, even an eight-foot problem. Sometimes things look so big and tall that it seems as if someone had placed a brick wall to block you and you cannot see your way through or around it. Don't give up. There is another way. Remember that when your back is against a wall, just walk forward. (See artwork, "Just Walk Forward.")

Zacchaeus looked over and saw a sycamore tree. He believed, 'If I just climb this tree, I will rise above my problems.' Zacchaeus began to rise. I can imagine him saying, 'I'm now over my five-foot-eight problem, now over my six-foot-four problem, but I still cannot see Jesus.' Sometimes it takes a little more effort, and this is when your faith must kick in. Some of us give up at the first problem. The Bible says, "faith without works is dead" (James 2:26).

Just because Zacchaeus couldn't see Jesus, it didn't mean He wasn't there. Jesus is ever-present, so He is still right in the midst of you. Zacchaeus rose just a little bit higher and pulled up. When you are depressed, you have to move and do something. Play inspirational music, worship, repeat your voices of victory, go to see a Christian comedian perform, go shopping, call a positive friend, get some ice cream, do anything, but sit and mope. You have to pull up and get out of yourself. Don't you know self-pity will kill you, self-pity will destroy you, self-pity will make you turn back, self-pity will make you give up? But if you keep seeking Jesus, you will find Him because He is always there. God says, "I will never leave thee nor forsake thee" (Hebrews 13:5). How reassuring is that?

So Zacchaeus continued to climb over his eight-foot problem and was able to look down on his troubles. (They didn't seem so big anymore.) He rose above it, and that's when he could see Jesus! When you allow yourself to rise above it, you will see Jesus. Not only will you see Jesus, but Jesus will see you. Please know when you seek Jesus in your situations, He will see you.

The Bible says, "When Jesus came to the place, he looked up and saw him"—Zacchaeus. How many of you know that Jesus will come to your place?—that place of hurt, sickness, loneliness, rejection, emptiness, fear, that place where you ask, "Why?" that place of endless tears, the time when no one else knows you're crying, the time when you are masking your feelings so people, family, and church folk won't see your pain. Yes, wherever you are at this time of life, Jesus knows where you are.

Jesus told Zacchaeus to "make haste and come down; for today I must abide in your house." The Lord wants you to make haste when you are depressed, burdened, or in trouble. Make haste so He can abide with you, sup with you in the house of your heart. So look up, for the Lord is near. The Bible says, "Behold I stand at the door and knock: if any man hears my voice and opens the door, I will come in to him, and will sup with him, and he with me" (Revelation 3:20).

Jesus will always knock before He comes in because He is not rude. Jesus wants a one-on-one relationship. He wants to be intimate with you. Yes, just with you! The spirit of depression intrudes on everything that is hopeful. Depression is an unwelcomed guest.

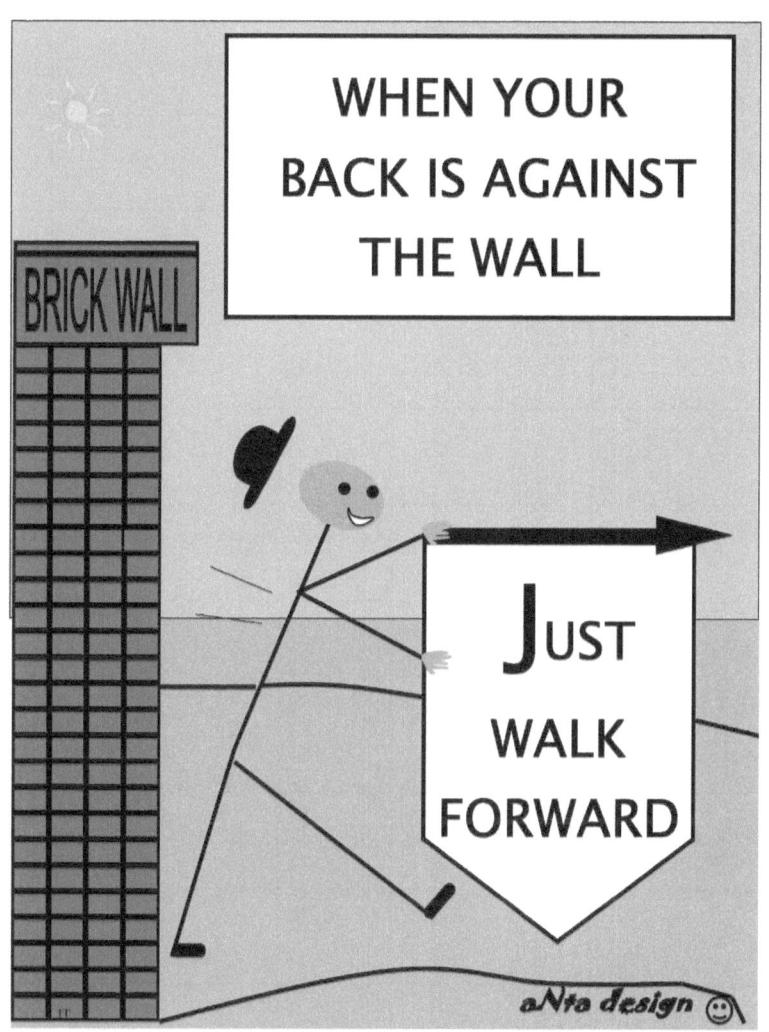

Reflections

(Use this page to write your innermost feelings, prayers, or thoughts.)

Date:_____

Chosen Scripture:_____

_____

_____

_____

_____

_____

_____

_____

_____

_____

Reflections

(Use this page to write your innermost feelings, prayers, or thoughts.)

Date:_____

Chosen Scripture:_____

_____

_____

_____

_____

_____

_____

_____

_____

_____

Reflections

(Use this page to write your innermost feelings, prayers, or thoughts.)

Date:_____

Chosen Scripture:_____

_____

_____

_____

_____

_____

_____

_____

_____

Reflections

(Use this page to write your innermost feelings, prayers, or thoughts.)

Date:_____

Chosen Scripture:_____

_____

_____

_____

_____

_____

_____

_____

_____

_____

Reflections

**(Use this page to write your innermost
feelings, prayers, or thoughts.)**

Date:_____

Chosen Scripture:_____

_____

_____

_____

_____

_____

_____

_____

_____

_____

CHAPTER 4

When You Don't Know What to Do

It is so important to know that when you don't know what to do, you can just worship. If you want to see depression tremble, just worship.

Here are four things worship does:

1. It acknowledges the greatness of God.
2. It admits the limitations of man.
3. It releases responsibility to God.
4. It disables the spirit of depression.

To lift up one's hands in worship and praise is not only giving God adoration, but lifting up one's desires and releasing what concerns us to God. Yes, the good, the bad and the ugly. Worshipping God gives Him recognition and gives Him overall authorization to intervene into our situations. By Worshipping and surrendering, you give up your will and your way. It's so important to worship. God is so merciful. By blessing the Lord, we end up with the benefits. God's benefits are from the air we breathe to His favor that is bestowed on us. The Bible says, "Blessed be the Lord, who daily loadeth us with benefits, even the God of our salvation" (Psalm 68:19).

Expressing the joy of the Lord can transform your mind, heart, and soul. It can actually change your attitude towards a crisis or situation happening in your life. Remember that when you worship, you are releasing yourself to the responsibility of God. You can say, "God, You can take it!". God wants us to lay our burdens on Him. "Casting all your care upon him; for he careth for you" (1 Peter 5:7).

Depression has no love for joy. Joy and depression cannot stay in the same house (your body). So we're going to serve this negative tenant an eviction notice right now, and tell it, "You are not welcome here! Not in my house! Leave in the name of Jesus!" Now, you can praise God.

We must worship the Lord in spirit and in truth. People can lift up their hands to God and imitate you in service, but the true worshippers worship the Lord because they love him and trust him.

The Lord has shown me a vision of what takes place when we are in true worship. In the vision, I saw a congregation of believers with their hands outstretched, yielding themselves to God. As they were surrendering their will, it looked like raindrops going upward from their bodies, and each drop had a name: depression, hurt, pain, heartbreak, foreclosure, children, divorce, grief and many more concerns.

As you worship, you are emptying and releasing whatever it is to the Lord, so that He can deposit back to you what you need. This is why you feel so relieved, refreshed and even renewed after you worship. Worshipping puts you in a place alone with God even when there are thousands of worshippers around you. Worshipping is a one-on-one experience: no kids, no husband, no wife, no limitations, and no one else but God and you up close and personal. Just be real with God. In other words, say how you truly feel. Don't be afraid. We read in the Bible that David was so truthful with his feelings that God said, "I have found David, the son of Jesse, a man after My own heart" (Acts 13:22). Remember that God already knows your feelings, so be truthful. It's all right!

Two words are so powerful that they move God. Do you know what they are? These words are "Thank you."

There was a time in my life I was so sick in bed that I could not move and didn't know when it would ever end. I felt so alone and sorry for myself, even though there were people in almost every room of the house. I felt so weak that I could not even think of what to be thankful for, so I looked toward my vanity and began thanking God for the things on my vanity. "Lord, I thank You for my brush, my comb, the mirror, and every drawer. Lord, I thank You for my blanket." Before I knew it, my words of thanks became so sincere I could feel again. I threw my blanket off, jumped out of my bed, and continued to bless the name of Jesus! Nothing but continuous praise of thanksgiving came out of my mouth. Then something happened. I felt the healing waters of Jesus flowing through my body. I was healed, restored, renewed, and refreshed, and I hadn't even taken my bath yet.

If you ever don't know what to do, start with this: "Lord, I thank You." If you don't know what to thank Him for, just start with something around your house or where you are, and if you are still having a problem, say, "Lord, I thank You for the breath in my body." The words, *thank you,* moves God.

I have a granddaughter named Kyndall. (Yes, she's my heart.). When I give her a toddler's treat, she says, "Thank you, Grandma." It's something in the way she says it and the way she looks at me with the most grateful, loving, and appreciative eyes. It touches my heart. It moves me to do more. How much more will our heavenly Father do for us, His creation? The Bible says, "Fear not, little flock; for it is your Father's good pleasure to give you the kingdom" (Luke 12:32).

Reflections

(Use this page to write your innermost feelings, prayers, or thoughts.)

Date:_____

Chosen Scripture:_____

_____

_____

_____

_____

_____

_____

_____

_____

_____

Reflections

(Use this page to write your innermost feelings, prayers, or thoughts.)

Date:_____

Chosen Scripture:_____

_____

_____

_____

_____

_____

_____

_____

_____

_____

Reflections

**(Use this page to write your innermost
feelings, prayers, or thoughts.)**

Date:_____

Chosen Scripture:_____

_____

_____

_____

_____

_____

_____

_____

_____

_____

Reflections

(Use this page to write your innermost feelings, prayers, or thoughts.)

Date:_____

Chosen Scripture:_____

_____

_____

_____

_____

_____

_____

_____

_____

_____

Reflections

(Use this page to write your innermost feelings, prayers, or thoughts.)

Date:_____

Chosen Scripture:_____

_____

_____

_____

_____

_____

_____

_____

_____

_____

CHAPTER 5

This Is God's Glory Stuff

Revelation 12:12 says, "The devil is come down unto you, having great wrath, because he knoweth that he hath but a short time." This is why he's conducting such havoc, dividing families and running buck wild on earth.

The Bible says, "Do not worry about tomorrow because tomorrow will take care of itself" (Matthew 6:34 NIV). I remember one night I tossed and turned, worrying about a meeting that was going to take place on my job. I felt sick to my stomach, and I didn't get any sleep that night. When I walked in the office the next morning, I was told the person I feared would be out for at least three months. I worried about tomorrow for nothing. Tomorrow will come whether you worry or not, so why choose to worry. Place it in God's hands. It's His day anyway. Usually what you think is going to happen more than likely will not.

So turn over, relax, go to sleep, and allow God to meet you in His next day. Just remember the day is already His. "This is the day that the Lord has made; let us rejoice and be glad in it." The Lord was in your yesterday; He is meeting you today, and He will wait for you tomorrow. In other words, the Lord has been where you're going and is already there to welcome you with open arms. The Bible says, "Jesus Christ is the same yesterday, today, and forever" (Hebrews 13:8). He is ever-present.

I have an aunt who makes the best pound cakes. She knows exactly how much butter, eggs, sugar, and milk and all of the other ingredients that are necessary to get her result, which is a delicious, mouth-watering pound cake. Because God has made the perfect day, He tells us to rejoice and be glad in it. He will not put any more on us than we can bear. I know you heard this before, but really think about what you thought you could not bear, but God worked it out. With God, nothing is too hard or impossible. Remember you are not alone in this battle. When the battle is bigger, the victory is sweeter. "Behold, I am the Lord, the God of all flesh. Is there anything too hard for Me?" (Jeremiah 32:27). The answer is always *no.*

God does not get the glory out of what is easy or what you can do for yourself. God gets the glory out of those things that don't make sense or seem impossible to man. It makes no sense for Jesus to be able to feed five thousand people, not including women and children, with just two fish and five loaves of bread. *However, He did!* It makes no sense for Jesus turning water into wine. *However, He did!* It makes no sense for Jesus to call a dead man to come forth from his grave. *However, He did!* It makes no sense for the Red

Sea to part and the Israelites to walk across on dry land. *However, it happened!* It makes no sense Jesus was hung on the cross from which He could have come down at any time, but He stayed because God must get the glory. In other words, no one else can take His credit or glory. Man is placed in a position to recognize that "it is God and nobody else, but God and God alone."

Yes, glory stuff!

Reflections

(Use this page to write your innermost feelings, prayers, or thoughts.)

Date:_____

Chosen Scripture:_____

_____

_____

_____

_____

_____

_____

_____

_____

_____

Reflections

(Use this page to write your innermost feelings, prayers, or thoughts.)

Date:_____

Chosen Scripture:_____

_____

_____

_____

_____

_____

_____

_____

_____

_____

Reflections

(Use this page to write your innermost feelings, prayers, or thoughts.)

Date:_____

Chosen Scripture:_____

_____

_____

_____

_____

_____

_____

_____

_____

_____

Reflections

(Use this page to write your innermost feelings, prayers, or thoughts.)

Date:_____

Chosen Scripture:_____

_____

_____

_____

_____

_____

_____

_____

_____

_____

Reflections

(Use this page to write your innermost feelings, prayers, or thoughts.)

Date:_____

Chosen Scripture:_____

_____

_____

_____

_____

_____

_____

_____

_____

_____

CHAPTER 6

I Will Joy

Habakkuk: 3:17-19 says,

> Although the fig tree shall not blossom, neither shall fruit be in the vines; the labor of the olive shall fail and the fields shall yield no meat; the flock shall be cut off from the fold, and there shall be no herd in the stalls: Yet I will rejoice in the Lord, I will joy in the God of my salvation. The Lord God is my strength, and he will make my feet like hind's feet and He will make me to walk upon mine high places.

Habakkuk is saying this to us loud and clear. Yes, life sometimes can be unfair. The very thing we have cried about and prayed about seems as if it's not going to happen. The seeds we've planted take forever to grow. Our hearts' desires are seemingly broken into pieces. The world seems as if it's coming down on you with the true reality of what is happening in your life. However, in the midst of it all, don't lose your hope. Don't lose your trust in God. Verse 18 says, "Yet I will rejoice in the Lord!" In other words I choose to override my situation with praise. The use of the word yet changed the whole course and direction of Habakkuk's feelings and mood. It took his mind off of what he saw, and that allowed him to enter into a place of praise and trust.

I personally can tell you this *yet* stuff works. After I had written this book, I experienced a week of back-to-back, out-of-nowhere, and out-of-my-control events in my life. The emotional roller coaster was making me sick to my stomach. Then the phone rang. I was hoping it wasn't for me, but it was. Moreover, that news was just unbearable. It seemed as if it wouldn't stop, so I ran upstairs to my room and jumped in the bed. I threw the cover over my head and thought, *Lord, how much more? How much more?* Then I began to think on this book and started to follow what I like to call the "Yet Principle".

I began to list all the craziness that had happened to me like Habakkuk did in verse 17. Then I said loudly, "*Yet* I will rejoice in the Lord!" I said this over and over again until I jumped out of the same bed. I felt light. God had renewed my strength and restored something inside of me. I can't explain it, but I knew I could go on. I realized this had to be one of the exercises you could do to combat the enemy. Life will throw one thing after another at us, but we are prepared and ready with the Word of God.

Notice here that Habakkuk didn't say, "I will enjoy". He said, "I will joy". Why *joy*? Because joy is something you have inside of you. It's your very own. The world didn't give it to you, and the world cannot take it away. I chose to joy in the Lord, for the joy of the Lord is my strength and believe me, the devil knows it. This is why it is so important to praise and give God worship so you can *enjoy* God.

Have you ever seen those *Wild Kingdom* shows where the hind (a red female deer) is standing on a mountain and leaps from mountain cliff to mountain cliff? When she is threatened by the enemy, she just leaps without the thought of falling. Therefore, when the enemy thinks he has you, God makes your feet like hind's feet to escape to a higher place of safety in Him. The Lord will give you a way to escape and will place you where you should be, namely on a solid rock, and we know who that is. It may not be in your timing, but don't worry. It's God who has the ultimate check-off list to cover every detail of your life. In other words, He knows our future, and the devil is fearful of that. The Bible says, "For I know the plans I have for you, declares the Lord, plans to prosper you and not harm you, plans to give you hope and a future" (Jeremiah 29:11 NIV).

When the spirit of depression raises its ugly head and whispers in your ear, find a song to sing. Yes, have a joyous song of victory ready on the back burner of your heart. Lift your head up and move to the rhythm to let this negative spirit know that it is not welcomed and that it will not be received. It will soon get the message that you are "more than a conqueror" through Jesus Christ (Romans 8:37).

There are times when I'm at home alone and feel a downer coming on. At those times, I just break out into what I call a *joy bounce.* Yes, right in the midst of my storm, I joy-bounce. All you do is bend your knees a little, bounce, bounce again, bounce three times in a row, and push your shoulders upward with your arms and hands moving in the air while you bounce. Then repeat the process. Now think about the goodness of Jesus and praise Him. *It works!* The only catch is that you have to smile! You can't joy-bounce without smiling. Put on some gospel or inspirational music, and you're good to go. Remember the spirit of depression does not like joy. Your smile is God-given. Don't allow the devil to have it. God has personally designed it for you. A smile is contagious, so pass it on.

Reflections

(Use this page to write your innermost feelings, prayers, or thoughts.)

Date:_____

Chosen Scripture:_____

_____

_____

_____

_____

_____

_____

_____

_____

_____

Reflections

**(Use this page to write your innermost
feelings, prayers, or thoughts.)**

Date:_____

Chosen Scripture:_____

_____

_____

_____

_____

_____

_____

_____

_____

_____

Reflections

(Use this page to write your innermost feelings, prayers, or thoughts.)

Date:_____

Chosen Scripture:_____

_____

_____

_____

_____

_____

_____

_____

_____

_____

Reflections

(Use this page to write your innermost feelings, prayers, or thoughts.)

Date:_____

Chosen Scripture:_____

_____

_____

_____

_____

_____

_____

_____

_____

_____

_____

Reflections

(Use this page to write your innermost feelings, prayers, or thoughts.)

Date:_____

Chosen Scripture:_____

_____

_____

_____

_____

_____

_____

_____

_____

_____

CHAPTER 7

Don't Entertain Mr. and Mrs. Nobody

I know personally what the Mr. and Mrs. Nobody will do if you open the door and let them in. Trust me, if you allow them to come in they are going to bring the whole clan in with them. There was a time in my life when I never thought about weight gain and if I gained weight, I just had to say, "Ten pounds be gone," and they were gone! However, as soon as I hit my fifties, my weight put up a resistance. The battle of the bugle was winning the war. I thought if I announced it publicly, something miraculous would happen, so I told my husband. (By the way, he has no faith in me at all. I can't really blame him). I've been saying for years, "I'm going on a diet, honey." I joined a gym and still ended up in the same dress size. I told my sisters, my son, my church, even my two-year-old granddaughter, "I am going to lose weight." I tried everything, even this drink that stated, "If you drink this stuff for two days, you will lose ten pounds." Well, it's been two years, and I'm still waiting.

I allowed my weight to define who I had become. I was somewhere in there, and I had to find me again and nobody else could do that for me, but me. By the way, *nobody else* is the cousin to the *nobodies.* Nobody else is going through this but me. Nobody else is this size. Nobody else is being treated like this. Nobody else will help. Nobody else can. Nobody else will. *Stop!* You have just entered the "woe-is-me" syndrome. This is the voice of depression speaking, not you. It sneaks up on you in disguise to make you think these are your thoughts. Wrong! You're ready this time, so turn back to the voice of victory page and speak the voice of victory. This is how you disable the voice of depression in its tracks before it gets into your spirit.

I know that I'm overweight, and sometimes I can't tell if my body is coming or going; however, I'm still Nadine and I still love me. In fact, I like me. It is so important to like yourself. Therefore, go on with your big girl self and love who you are. I am not saying you should not lose weight. You still have to take care of yourself and do what is best for you. So go ahead and buy those new shoes; get your hair done (maybe change the style), and get a new dress. Just be the best you can be, as you seek out a weight-loss program that will fit your lifestyle. Note that losing weight is good for your health. There is no miracle pill. There is only God and your will to make a change.

If you consider being overweight an issue, this will give the nobodies just something else to use to bring you to despair. The hardest part of any change, diet, or any workout program is getting started. So get started. Make today your first day in the path toward a new you, and focus on being in good health.

Because of my weight, I felt like a nobody, and it almost convinced me to give up and believe there was nothing that would work for me. Guess what? I'm still overweight, but a change has been made in my mind. Yes, I changed my mind-set. The Bible says, "Let this mind be in you which is also in Christ Jesus" (Philippians 2:5). I realized even though I prayed to God for help in this matter, it's also my responsibility too. There are some things I have to change in my life: like getting my hands out of the potato chip bag, getting up from the couch and putting the remote control down. I have to stop watching my exercise tapes while lying down in the bed. No one can tell you to lose weight. No one can make you. No one can make your mind up for you. Does this sound familiar? Well, it's true. No one but *you*! There's someone else you cannot entertain— "Mr. I Can't!"

When you feel like you're a nobody, the answer is simple. *Don't!* The nobody feeling is dangerous! This is one feeling you don't want to sit down with at the kitchen table and serve a cup of hot coffee. It will spill it on you! The nobody syndrome has an eraser and wishes to slowly remove from your memory everything you have accomplished and achieved, the people you have touched, and those who love you. The devil is a liar! The Bible says, "Before you were ever formed in your mother's womb, I saw you and approved you" (Jeremiah 1:5 NIV).

No one needs to validate you because God has already approved you. Yes, you! You are God's gift for the purposes that you serve. You are the somebody God needs. No one can do it as uniquely as you can. Go on with your unique self. Go ahead right now, look in the mirror, and tell yourself that you are "fearfully and wonderfully made", that God does not make junk and that you are more than a conqueror! Hold your head up, shoulders back, stand tall, and walk forward. You are that somebody the world needs to know, and I thank God for you.

Please know it's all right to need someone. It's all right to ask someone for help. The Bible says, "Ask, and it shall be given you; seek, and ye shall find; knock, and it shall be opened unto you" (Matthew 7:7). That someone can be just the person in your life to intercede for you, hold you up in prayer, and support you. The list goes on and on. Don't let the nobodies confuse you so that you believe that "it's me, myself, and I that will simply open the door to the nobodies."

It is my belief that by the time this book is published, I will be at my desired weight. We can pray all we want to, but we have to do something to start the process. It takes work; so work we shall do. Let's do this together. We can do all things through Jesus Christ. Don't quit on me or yourself. Let's do this! I feel better already. Smile!

I claim the victory over us and declare, "Today, the 'nobodies' in us die, and the 'somebodies' come forward and live."

Reflections

(Use this page to write your innermost feelings, prayers, or thoughts.)

Date:_____

Chosen Scripture:_____

_____

_____

_____

_____

_____

_____

_____

_____

_____

Reflections

(Use this page to write your innermost feelings, prayers, or thoughts.)

Date:_____

Chosen Scripture:_____

_____

_____

_____

_____

_____

_____

_____

_____

_____

Reflections

(Use this page to write your innermost feelings, prayers, or thoughts.)

Date:_____

Chosen Scripture:_____

_____

_____

_____

_____

_____

_____

_____

_____

_____

Reflections

**(Use this page to write your innermost
feelings, prayers, or thoughts.)**

Date:_____

Chosen Scripture:_____

_____

_____

_____

_____

_____

_____

_____

_____

Reflections

(Use this page to write your innermost feelings, prayers, or thoughts.)

Date:_____

Chosen Scripture:_____

_____

_____

_____

_____

_____

_____

_____

_____

_____

CHAPTER 8

So You Want Peace—Really?

My life's experiences have made me realize that peace has no backbone. That's right. It's yellow. As soon as there's trouble, peace takes a hike. Just imagine you're at home and minding your own business, happy as can be. Then out of nowhere there's a knock at your door, and your neighbor screams, "A truck has just hit your car." Peace is gone!

To prove this point even more, there's a story in the Bible about Jesus being in a boat crossing the sea with His disciples. After a tiring day, Jesus went to sleep in the back of the boat. A great storm of wind arose. The boat was filling up with water, tossing them from side to side. The disciples were very frightened and didn't understand how Jesus could sleep so peacefully through what looked like doom to them. They said to Jesus, "Don't you even care that we perish?"

Jesus woke up and just said, "Peace, be still." See, perfect peace (Jesus) had to tell *peace* to stand still. In other words Jesus said, "Peace, you cannot go anywhere unless I say so. Just behave yourself and know who I am—perfect peace."

I know sometimes you feel like this boat. In addition, sometimes you not only feel like this boat, but you *are* the boat. Life has you all filled up with tears. The winds of life have you tossing and turning all night.

You're worried about yesterday's struggles with no solutions for tomorrow. You are afraid of what steps or decisions to make. You understand the feeling of being surrounded, with nowhere to go because any direction you might take is a long way down.

Well, I bring you good news. Jesus is on board your boat. He sees all that stuff (cargo/baggage) you are carrying across your sea of life, sometimes through no fault of your own, as sometimes life can be so unfair.

Just like in this story, things in life can happen so abruptly, giving us no warning. However, this type of situation happens and our Lord does His best work. We must realize that Jesus hears us when we call and He will answer that which concerns us. These stories in the Word of God weren't placed there just for historical purposes. We can use these stories as promises and principles to live our daily lives. They can remind us of who God is and what He can do to help us navigate through every storm that we must pass through. The Bible says, "All scripture is given by inspiration of God, and is profitable for doctrine, for reproof, for correction, for instruction in righteousness" (II Timothy 3:16).

Now that we have a better understanding of peace, let's say this together, "Don't ask for peace—instead, ask for perfect peace." Therefore, I declare today that Jesus Christ's perfect peace will be with you and surround you and your family with its tender care and love. My friends, peace has left the building, but perfect peace is still here. Be encouraged! In Jesus' name ... Amen. Praise God!

Reflections

(Use this page to write your innermost feelings, prayers, or thoughts.)

Date:_____

Chosen Scripture:_____

_____

_____

_____

_____

_____

_____

_____

_____

_____

Reflections

(Use this page to write your innermost feelings, prayers, or thoughts.)

Date:_____

Chosen Scripture:_____

_____

_____

_____

_____

_____

_____

_____

_____

_____

Reflections

(Use this page to write your innermost feelings, prayers, or thoughts.)

Date:_____

Chosen Scripture:_____

_____

_____

_____

_____

_____

_____

_____

_____

_____

_____

Reflections

(Use this page to write your innermost feelings, prayers, or thoughts.)

Date:_____

Chosen Scripture:_____

_____

_____

_____

_____

_____

_____

_____

_____

_____

Reflections

(Use this page to write your innermost feelings, prayers, or thoughts.)

Date:_____

Chosen Scripture:_____

_____

_____

_____

_____

_____

_____

_____

_____

_____

CHAPTER 9

On Your Mark, Get Ready, Set, and Go! You Already Won!

There is a television show that I have watched from time to time called *Minute To Win It*, and the host begins each show by asking each contestant are they "In It to Win It?" My coincidence I was asked to speak on this very theme. So I thought and pondered on this topic and scripture. It was coming from Hebrews 12:1-2, which says,

> Wherefore seeing we also are compassed about with so great a cloud of witnesses, let us lay aside every weight, and the sin which doth so easily beset us, and let us run with patience the race that is set before us, looking unto Jesus the author and finisher of our faith; who for the joy that was set before him endured the cross, despising the shame, and is set down at the right hand of the throne of God.

The questions become these: "What are you *in*, and what will you *win*?" If you have accepted Jesus Christ as your Savior, confess with your mouth that Jesus is Lord, and repent from your sins, take off the old man (get rid of old habits), put on the new and claim to be redeemed. If you are able to check off any of the above, then I say congratulations, because you are now in it. You are in the race.

The good news is that Jesus is still the Alpha and Omega, the beginning and the end, and if He is at the beginning of a thing, He is also at the end. The Word says, "He is the author and finisher of our faith." Jesus was there when you started this race, and He will be there when you finish. Therefore, we have to deal with all of the in-between stuff in this race. That's why I believe Hebrews 12:1 likens our journey as running a race, because God knew we would race against time, doubt, hopelessness, sickness, temptation, hurts, despair, fear and other challenges.

The race we're in goes all the way back to Genesis when Adam and Eve ate of the forbidden fruit from the tree of good and evil. The first thing that was affected was their sight. The Bible says that their eyes were opened and they realized that they were naked; and so today the devil is still trying to get God's people to look at their circumstances, situations, finances, hopelessness, sickness, discouragement, disappointments, and the things that are just out of our control. So we lose our focus and forget that our main goal is to win this race. That's why God in His infinite wisdom told us in His Word to "walk by faith and not by sight." He said that so that we would not see the things that the devil has placed before us, but would totally trust Him. See, our reality is not God's, because with Him nothing is impossible and this is how He wants us to run this race.

The devil cannot run this race with you because he is not redeemed. His destiny is sealed. So he is angry and makes it his job to place things before you, stop you, cause interference, block, trip, and blindside you so you will lose focus. So let's tell the devil, "I'm in it to win it!"

The Bible says in Hebrews 12:1, "Let us lay aside every weight." About two years ago I was working out with a personal trainer. We were jogging along when we came to a very high hill, and she said, "Okay, put on these ankle weights and take the hill." Yes, I looked at her as if she was crazy, but I obeyed and started up the hill. Of course, she was ahead of me. I complained all the way up the hill, "I can't do this. I'm not going to make it. My legs are going to give out. Can I stop now?" I finally reached the top, and we continued to run until we reached another very high hill, and she said, "Okay, take off the ankle weights." I was happy to hear those words, so I took them off, and I went up the hill with such ease. See, when you lay aside every weight and when you let something go, God can put something in.

Consider the following:

- If you lay aside depression, you pick up joy.
- If you lay aside fear, you pick up confidence.

- If you lay aside sin, you pick up salvation.
- If you lay aside grief, you pick up life.
- If you lay aside battles, you pick up victory.
- If you lay aside hopelessness, you pick up faith.
- If you lay aside trouble, you pick up peace.
- If you lay aside hate, you pick up love.
- If you lay aside poor, you pick up wealth.
- If you lay aside blame, you pick up forgiveness.

If you lay aside the things that hinder you, you will be able to take the hill and be free to move forward in God and in your life's ambition. When I was murmuring and complaining about the weights, I couldn't hear my instructor. I forgot the reason we were there. I was undermining my own goals to lose weight, and I became my own worst enemy. When we murmur and complain, it prevents us from hearing and receiving instructions from God. When we don't continue on the straight and narrow path, we find ourselves all over the place, off track, and confused.

In Luke 8:43-48, we read about a woman who definitely was in it to win it. She was the woman with the issue of blood. She would bleed for twelve years, seeking doctor after doctor, with no cure or remedy and now no money. Can you imagine what she must have been going through? She probably wasn't invited to many social events or family reunions. She had this sickness not for six months or eight years; but for twelve years she suffered with this condition. What if she had stopped trying? What if she had felt sorry for herself and sat on the edge of her bed, staring out her window? She would have never met Jesus, the one she so needed.

She didn't allow her condition. or what people were thinking or saying about her to hold her back. She pressed her way to reach the source of her healing and wholeness. She never gave up, and you cannot give up either. She trusted Jesus and didn't doubt. She touched the hem of His garment and His healing virtue connected to her faith and released to her wholeness and peace.

I can only imagine what you are going through or experiencing right now, but I want you to know that just like the woman with the issue of blood you can't give up. You're in it to win it.

God's hands personally designed you for His purpose. Who would have known that this woman's story, which happened more than two thousand years ago, would still touch hearts and encourage God's people not to quit the race until they reach their desired goals. She didn't know at that time how important her place would be in history and the effect she would have on so many of God's people. This is what the devil wants to hide from you—your importance to the body of Christ, the many things you have accomplished, and the people you have blessed and touched. You may not get all the accolades or the standing ovations, but you should know that God sees and is keeping record and all will be worth it.

Who knows what stories people are telling about you—perhaps about something you said to encourage them or something you did that changed their lives— and they passed that story on to others to bless them. In other words you are making your own history and may not even be aware of it. All you have to do is live, and God will do the rest.

I enjoy watching the Olympics, especially the races where people from all over the world represent their countries in competition. They may run different races, but they all have the same goal—to win. They have to be committed to their assigned races, and no one can run it for them. This is why the Word refers to "the race that is set before us." We have to run our own race. My race will not be like yours, and yours will not be like mine.

The race of life comes with all types of challenges. We don't choose many of these challenges, so we must run this race with patience and endurance. Don't lose your focus. Maintain your commitment and passion at a high level, and they will keep you from giving up when the race gets rough.

I remember in 1992 I was watching the Barcelona Olympic races when a British athlete was running a relay race. When he was no more than 250 meters from the finish line, he injured his hamstring, but he did not stop running. He began to hop along toward the finish line. It looked like he was not going to make it to the end of the race, but he just kept hopping along. Then all of a sudden, his father came from out of nowhere and lifted him up, and together they walked to the finish line. This runner did not win the race, but he won a personal victory. The Bible says in Ecclesiastes 9:11, "The race is not to the swift, nor the battle to the strong," and in Matthew 24:13, "but he that shall endure to the end." It's not how fast you run; it's how well you run. Even if you're weak in this race and fall down, you have a heavenly Father who will leave His throne to hold you up with His right hand.

You must endure until the end if you expect to hear Jesus say, "Well done, my good and faithful servant. You have been faithful over a few things. I will make

you ruler over many. Enter into the joy of the Lord"
(Matthew 25:21). You are in this race to win it, and
you will.

As we run this race, God has given us a reminder
in Hebrews 12:1, which says, "Wherefore seeing we
also are compassed about with so great a cloud of
witnesses."

This scripture clearly tells us that we are not alone,
but Hebrews 11 actually tells us who are cheering
us on as we run this race—all those who have been
faithful and stood the test of time and have gone on
before us, those who came through the fire and did
not burn, those who crossed the Red Sea on dry
land, and those who endured imprisonment and were
miraculously set free. Because they kept the faith, they
now surround us as clouds to remind us that we can
make it too. When you see the clouds of witnesses in
the sky cheering you on, remember they are Moses,
Noah, Shadrach, Meshach, Abednego, Apostle Paul,
Sara, Rahab, Ruth, Naomi, Abel, Abraham, Isaac, and
Jacob, just to name a few.

So when you're standing alone at a bus stop or sitting
on your bed of depression or staring out of your car
window, just look up and see the clouds above and
remember you are not in this race alone. There are

those who have gone before you to encourage you to keep moving. They are saying, "You can make it. Don't give up. You're too close to turn around. You're almost there. This is not your battle, and victory is yours."

Just stay the course because God has much more in store for you than this world can begin to offer. You will make it to the finish line, and in God's eyes you are already a winner. As a matter of fact, I just heard Him say to you, "Well done."

Reflections

(Use this page to write your innermost feelings, prayers, or thoughts.)

Date:_____

Chosen Scripture:_____

_____

_____

_____

_____

_____

_____

_____

_____

_____

Reflections

(Use this page to write your innermost feelings, prayers, or thoughts.)

Date:_____

Chosen Scripture:_____

_____

_____

_____

_____

_____

_____

_____

_____

_____

Reflections

**(Use this page to write your innermost
feelings, prayers, or thoughts.)**

Date:_____

Chosen Scripture:_____

_____

_____

_____

_____

_____

_____

_____

_____

_____

Reflections

(Use this page to write your innermost feelings, prayers, or thoughts.)

Date:_____

Chosen Scripture:_____

_____

_____

_____

_____

_____

_____

_____

_____

_____

Reflections

(Use this page to write your innermost feelings, prayers, or thoughts.)

Date:_____

Chosen Scripture:_____

_____

_____

_____

_____

_____

_____

_____

_____

CHAPTER 10

A Personal Word for Women and Men

Women, note your menstrual cycles. At this time when the blood is low, the spirit of depression can really talk to you and bring you down. So it is important to recognize it and say, "Okay, I'm only feeling this way because it's that time of month. I'm fine in Jesus' name." This is only temporary. Remember it is this spirit's job to make you think it's worse than it really is.

Men, do not bite off more than you can chew. It's okay to ask for help. Don't be so hard on yourselves. God is your head, so look to Him.

Men and women should find a good faith base church, get plenty of rest, drink plenty of water, exercise, and associate with positive people. You should find someone you can talk to about anything and everything. You should also stay away from toxic people, as they are whiners, downers, gossipers, the self-pitying folks, and those people who generally don't have anything good to say about anyone. If you have not done this, make an appointment with your health care provider for a complete physical. You should remember to delegate as much as you can, especially if you're in the ministry.

It's all right to cry. Psalm 34:17 says, "The righteous cry, and the Lord heareth, and delivereth them out of all their troubles." Who will cry? The righteous will, but God will hear and deliver. You can depend on His Word.

I believe these things will help: Learn to recognize this spirit of depression through its voice and begin to disable it with words of praise, thanksgiving, and confidence; treat yourself from time to time; you deserve it; go to a Christian comedy show; take the pill of laughter; you may not need anything else; laughter is medicine; do not take things so seriously, and know that God will meet you in your tomorrow; do not let the devil take away that right from you; and most of all, learn to laugh at yourself.

Parents, you can use this book as a study guide for your children. Help them to be prepared for this spirit of depression. Let them know that they can always come to you when they have these down feelings that they don't understand. Help them to know the voice of depression and the voice of victory. Remind them often of their accomplishments, no matter how small, and let them know they're not alone. Moms and dads, if you see your children sad, don't overlook it. Ask questions, have compassion, and don't let them lock themselves in their rooms. Go in, hug them, and let them know there is nothing that you and God can't handle. Assure them that there will always be a new dawning and things won't always be the same. If a psychiatrist is needed, don't hesitate to seek one. Don't let what you think people will say or what you think get in the way of you and your child's health. If your child came to you with a broken leg, would you not take him/her to a physician or specialist for help?

I rest my case.

Reflections

(Use this page to write your innermost feelings, prayers, or thoughts.)

Date:_____

Chosen Scripture:_____

_____

_____

_____

_____

_____

_____

_____

_____

Reflections

(Use this page to write your innermost feelings, prayers, or thoughts.)

Date:_____

Chosen Scripture:_____

_____

_____

_____

_____

_____

_____

_____

_____

_____

Reflections

(Use this page to write your innermost feelings, prayers, or thoughts.)

Date:_____

Chosen Scripture:_____

_____

_____

_____

_____

_____

_____

_____

_____

_____

_____

Reflections

(Use this page to write your innermost feelings, prayers, or thoughts.)

Date:_____

Chosen Scripture:_____

_____

_____

_____

_____

_____

_____

_____

_____

_____

Reflections

(Use this page to write your innermost feelings, prayers, or thoughts.)

Date:_____

Chosen Scripture:_____

_____

_____

_____

_____

_____

_____

_____

_____

_____

CHAPTER 11

It's Okay to Seek a Physician. Yes, a Psychiatrist

Please listen. Forget about the taboo that is attached to seeing a psychiatrist. Don't we go to see a doctor for the flu, diabetes, heart attacks, strokes, and other illnesses? If you need physical therapy, do you not try to strengthen what is weak? If medical treatment is needed, don't hesitate to seek help. Don't let family, friends, or church folk get in the way of your family member's mental health.

I am now in my fifties, and in my life's journey, the spirit of depression has raised its ugly head from time to time. Through the years I had to endure many things—the shooting of my son, (thank God he lived), sickness, the deaths of my father and my mother, injustice in the workplace, hurt by church folk, broken relationships, even weight issues, and much more.

I am proud to say I sought a Christian psychiatrist. I learned so much from her. I learned that sometimes many overwhelming things can happen to a person at one time and can actually cause a chemical imbalance in the body. You can even suppress traumatic events so much that you don't even know they are affecting you and those around you.

Therefore, if you need to seek a physician/psychiatrist, do so with my blessing and with the Word of God. "He who is sick seeks a physician" (Matthew 9:12).

So take my book with you while you're in the doctor's reception room or waiting for the pills to chemically balance you. It will help you. Medications are not always prescribed; sometimes it is good to have someone who is professionally and spiritually trained to listen and keep what you're experiencing confidential. You won't have to look over your shoulders on Sunday. I recommend that you find a Christian psychiatrist or psychologist because he or she will not only recommend medicine, but can minister the word of God to you. A spirit-filled physician will see beyond your natural needs and speak to your spiritual needs as well.

I hope you have learned from the things that I have written in this book—how to recognize the voice of depression and the voice of victory; how to acknowledge the greatness of God; how to admit your limitations; how to release responsibility to God; and how to disable the spirit of depression. Make sure that you also give yourself the authority to dance in your storm.

Reflections

(Use this page to write your innermost
feelings, prayers, or thoughts.)

Date:_____

Chosen Scripture:_____

_____

_____

_____

_____

_____

_____

_____

_____

_____

Reflections

(Use this page to write your innermost feelings, prayers, or thoughts.)

Date: _____

Chosen Scripture: _____

_____

_____

_____

_____

_____

_____

_____

_____

_____

Reflections

(Use this page to write your innermost feelings, prayers, or thoughts.)

Date:_____

Chosen Scripture:_____

_____

_____

_____

_____

_____

_____

_____

_____

_____

Reflections

(Use this page to write your innermost feelings, prayers, or thoughts.)

Date:_____

Chosen Scripture:_____

_____

_____

_____

_____

_____

_____

_____

_____

_____

Reflections

(Use this page to write your innermost feelings, prayers, or thoughts.)

Date:_____

Chosen Scripture:_____

_____

_____

_____

_____

_____

_____

_____

_____

_____

CHAPTER 12

You Have the Authority

Dancing In The Storm

aNto design

When you hear the voice of depression speaking, quickly repeat the following:

No! That's not the voice of God.

There's nothing too hard for God.

I am strong.

God is with me.

I am not alone.

I bless Your name, God.

I am more than this.

I am not defeated.

I will make it.

God has not forgotten me.

I am more than a conqueror.

I bleed the blood of Jesus.

(There's something about bleeding the blood of
Jesus. It works!)

I have the favor of God resting on my shoulders.

I am blessed going in. I am blessed coming out.

Thank You!
Thank You!
Thank You!
Thank You!
Thank You!
Thank You!
Thank You!
Thank You!
Thank You!
God is with me!
God will never leave me.

Just as this page came out of nowhere, so does the
spirit of depression. I have repeated this page again in
chapter 14 so you can locate it quickly when you need
it. Feel free to make a copy. Keep it in your purse or
wallet and say it repeatedly until you have overridden
that feeling of doom or despair. It's not important that
you memorize all of these, but try to remember what
you can or, just keep repeating, "Lord, I thank You.

Lord, I thank You." Saying, "Lord, I thank You", especially when you're in the midst of your storm, is a weapon in itself. Use it and use it often. It works.

Today you must choose to be happy. (Sometimes this seems easier said than done, but it can be done.) Wake up every morning and say, "Hello, Jesus. What's Your plan for me today?" Have a song in your mouth. (Hum it as you dress for the day.) Memorize your favorite scripture.

Doing something for someone else will help to keep depression at bay. You can send a note of encouragement to someone, buy boxes of cereal for a family in your neighborhood, plan a movie night with friends, or volunteer to serve food at a homeless shelter. In other words, keep busy. Not only are these things very rewarding, but they will help keep you from moping, complaining, and feeling sorry for yourself.

Please know that God loves you. He wants you to be happy. He wants you to have life more abundantly. God desires you to prosper naturally and spiritually, so don't give up! If I had given up, I would not have seen the promises of God manifested in my life. Please know you are important, so you should choose to fight because you will win!

This spirit of depression is one of the many weapons that the adversary uses against God's people, but be ready and be prepared with God, who is on our side. The Bible says, "No weapon that is formed against thee shall prosper" (Isaiah 54:17).

Depression, you are defeated in Jesus' name. I do believe that deserves a joy bounce!

Reflections

**(Use this page to write your innermost
feelings, prayers, or thoughts.)**

Date:_____

Chosen Scripture:_____

_____

_____

_____

_____

_____

_____

_____

_____

_____

Reflections

(Use this page to write your innermost feelings, prayers, or thoughts.)

Date:_____

Chosen Scripture:_____

_____

_____

_____

_____

_____

_____

_____

_____

_____

Reflections

(Use this page to write your innermost feelings, prayers, or thoughts.)

Date:_____

Chosen Scripture:_____

_____

_____

_____

_____

_____

_____

_____

_____

_____

Reflections

(Use this page to write your innermost feelings, prayers, or thoughts.)

Date:_____

Chosen Scripture:_____

_____

_____

_____

_____

_____

_____

_____

_____

_____

Reflections

(Use this page to write your innermost feelings, prayers, or thoughts.)

Date:_____

Chosen Scripture:_____

_____

_____

_____

_____

_____

_____

_____

_____

_____

CHAPTER 13

Helpful Scriptures

Don't be afraid.

Fear thou not, for I am with thee: be not dismayed; for I am thy God: I will strengthen thee; yea, I will help thee; yea, I will uphold thee with the right hand of my righteousness.

—Isaiah 41:10

God is working.

And we know that all things work together for good to them that love God, to them who are the called according to His purpose.

—Romans 8:28

I will come to you.

I will not leave you comfortless: I will come to you.

—John 14:18

His song is with me.

Yet the Lord will command his loving-kindness in the daytime, and in the night his song shall be with me, and my prayer unto the God of my life.

—Psalm 42:8

He is perfect peace.

Thou wilt keep him in perfect peace, whose mind is stayed on thee: because he trusteth in thee.

—Isaiah 26:3

Bless the Lord.

I will bless the Lord at all times: his praise shall continually be in my mouth.

—Psalm 34:1

Be strong.

O man greatly beloved, fear not: peace be unto thee, be strong, yea be strong. And when he had spoken unto me, I was strengthened, and said; Let my Lord speak; for He has strengthened me.

—Daniel 10:19

When troubled, receive peace.

Peace I leave with you, my peace I give unto you: not as the world giveth, give I unto you. Let not your heart be troubled, neither let it be afraid.

—John 14:27

It's all right to cry.

The righteous cry, and the Lord heareth, and delivereth them out of all their troubles.

—Psalm 34:17

Sorrow turns to joy.

Therefore the redeemed of the Lord shall return, and come with singing unto Zion; and everlasting joy shall be upon their head: they shall obtain gladness and joy; and sorrow and mourning shall flee away.

—Isaiah 51:11

Power is given.

He giveth power to the faint; and to them that have no might he increaseth strength.

—Isaiah 40:29

I shall not want.

The Lord is my Shepherd I shall not want.

—Psalm 23:1

The Lord is my rock.

The Lord is my rock, and my fortress and my deliverer; my God, my strength, in whom I will trust; my buckler, and the horn of my salvation, and my high tower.

—Psalm 18:2

Sleep shall be sweet.

When thou liest down, thou shalt not be afraid: yea, thou shalt lie down, and thy sleep shall be sweet.

—Proverbs 3:24

God cares.

Casting all your care upon him; for he careth for you.

—1 Peter 5:7

Be of good courage.

Wait on the Lord; be of good courage, and he shall strengthen thine heart: wait, I say, on the Lord.

—Psalm 27:14

There is liberty.
Now the Lord is that Spirit: and where the Spirit of the Lord is there is Liberty.

—2 Corinthians 3:17

Stand up to evil.
Wherefore take unto you the whole armour of God, that ye may be able to withstand in the evil day, and having done all, to stand.

—Ephesians 6:13

Be Christ-minded.
Let this mind be in you, which was also in Christ Jesus.

—Philippians 2:5

With Thanksgiving, there is peace.
Be anxious for nothing; but in everything by prayer and supplication with thanksgiving let your requests be made known unto God. And the peace of God, which passeth all understanding, shall keep your hearts and minds through Christ Jesus.

—Philippians 4:6-7

The Lord has not forsaken you.
When my father and my mother forsake me, then the Lord will take me up.

—Psalm 27:10

Lift my head.

But thou, O Lord, art a shield for me; my glory, and the lifter up of mine head.

—Psalm 3:3

I trust You.

When I am afraid, I will trust in you

—Psalm 56:3

Be not weary.

And let us not be weary in well doing: for in due season we shall reap, if we faint not.

—Galatians 6:9

Pray without ceasing.

Pray without ceasing. In everything give thanks: for this is the will of God in Christ Jesus concerning you.

—1 Thessalonians 5:17-18

I will reap.

Those who sow in tears shall reap with songs of joy.

—Psalm 126:5

Restore.

For I will restore health unto thee, and I will heal thee of thy wounds, saith the Lord.

—Jeremiah 30:17

Nothing is too hard for God.

Behold, I am the Lord, the God of all flesh: is there anything too hard for me?

—Jeremiah: 32:27

Sickness needs a physician.

They that are whole need not a physician, but they that are sick.

—Matthew 9:12

The Lord will deliver.

Many are the affections of the righteous: but the Lord delivereth him out of them all.

—Psalm 34:19

There is a fiery trial.

Beloved, think it not strange concerning the fiery trial which is to try you, as though some strange thing happened unto you: But rejoice, inasmuch as ye are partakers of Christ's sufferings; that, when his glory shall be revealed, ye may be glad also with exceeding joy.

—1 Peter 4:12-13

God heals the broken heart.

He healeth the broken in heart, and bindeth up their wounds.

—Psalm 147:3

I will help thee.
For I the Lord thy God will hold thy right hand,
saying unto thee, Fear not; I will help thee.

—Isaiah 41:13

Behold, I stand.
I stand at the door, and knock: if any man hears my
voice, and opens the door; I will come into him, and
will sup with him, and he with me.

—Revelation 3:20

God will supply all your needs.
But my God shall supply all your need according to
his riches in glory by Christ Jesus.

—Philippians 4:19

Sing.
Sing and rejoice, O daughter of Zion for, lo I come
and I will dwell in the midst of thee, saith the Lord.

—Zechariah 2:10

Joy is strength.
For the joy of the Lord is your strength

—Nehemiah 8:10

You're approved.
Before you were ever formed in your mother's womb,
I saw you and approved you.

—Jeremiah 1:5

We are more than conquerors.

We are more than conquerors through him that loved us.

—Romans 8:37

Cheer up.

Anxiety in a man's heart weighs it down, but a good word cheers it up.

—Proverbs 12:25

Reflections

(Use this page to write your innermost feelings, prayers, or thoughts.)

Date:_____

Chosen Scripture:_____

_____

_____

_____

_____

_____

_____

_____

_____

_____

Reflections

**(Use this page to write your innermost
feelings, prayers, or thoughts.)**

Date: _____

Chosen Scripture: _____

_____

_____

_____

_____

_____

_____

_____

_____

_____

Reflections

(Use this page to write your innermost feelings, prayers, or thoughts.)

Date:_____

Chosen Scripture:_____

_____

_____

_____

_____

_____

_____

_____

_____

_____

Reflections

(Use this page to write your innermost feelings, prayers, or thoughts.)

Date:_____

Chosen Scripture:_____

_____

_____

_____

_____

_____

_____

_____

_____

_____

Reflections

(Use this page to write your innermost feelings, prayers, or thoughts.)

Date:_____

Chosen Scripture:_____

_____

_____

_____

_____

_____

_____

_____

_____

CHAPTER 14

When You Need Me

When you hear the voice of depression speaking, quickly repeat the following:

No! That's not the voice of God.

There's nothing too hard for God.

I am strong.

God is with me.

I am not alone.

I bless Your name, God.

I am more than this.

I am not defeated.

I will make it.

God has not forgotten me.

I am more than a conqueror.

I bleed the blood of Jesus.

(There's something about bleeding the blood of
Jesus. It works!)

I have the favor of God resting on my shoulders.

I am blessed going in. I am blessed coming out.

Thank You!
Thank You!
Thank You!
Thank You!
Thank You!
Thank You!
Thank You!
God is with me.
God will never leave me.

Reflections

(Use this page to write your innermost feelings, prayers, or thoughts.)

Date:_____

Chosen Scripture:_____

_____

_____

_____

_____

_____

_____

_____

_____

_____

Reflections

(Use this page to write your innermost feelings, prayers, or thoughts.)

Date:_____

Chosen Scripture:_____

_____

_____

_____

_____

_____

_____

_____

_____

_____

Reflections

**(Use this page to write your innermost
feelings, prayers, or thoughts.)**

Date:_____

Chosen Scripture:_____

_____

_____

_____

_____

_____

_____

_____

_____

_____

Reflections

**(Use this page to write your innermost
feelings, prayers, or thoughts.)**

Date:_____

Chosen Scripture:_____

_____

_____

_____

_____

_____

_____

_____

_____

_____

Reflections

(Use this page to write your innermost feelings, prayers, or thoughts.)

Date:_____

Chosen Scripture:_____

_____

_____

_____

_____

_____

_____

_____

_____

_____

God's Got-It Envelope

Get a blank envelope and mark on it, "God's Got It." As the Word says, "My help comes from the Lord," so when you have certain concerns or worries, write them down on a piece paper and place it in your "God's got-it" envelope and put it away in your Bible or a private place. My envelope is under my bed. (Oh, well, I guess that's no longer private.). Now leave it there. Go about your day, hopefully stress-free, and if you think about it (your concern) again, just say, "God's got it!" When you place a concern in the envelope, see yourself placing it in God's hands. Trust God, who not only made heaven and earth but created that special person (you). If you wish, go ahead and joy-bounce!

Reflections

(Use this page to write your innermost
feelings, prayers, or thoughts.)

Date:_____

Chosen Scripture:_____

_____

_____

_____

_____

_____

_____

_____

_____

Reflections

(Use this page to write your innermost
feelings, prayers, or thoughts.)

Date:_____

Chosen Scripture:_____

_____

_____

_____

_____

_____

_____

_____

_____

_____

Reflections

(Use this page to write your innermost
feelings, prayers, or thoughts.)

Date:_____

Chosen Scripture:_____

_____

_____

_____

_____

_____

_____

_____

_____

_____

Reflections

(Use this page to write your innermost
feelings, prayers, or thoughts.)

Date:_____

Chosen Scripture:_____

_____

_____

_____

_____

_____

_____

_____

_____

_____

Reflections

(Use this page to write your innermost
feelings, prayers, or thoughts.)

Date:_____

Chosen Scripture:_____

_____

_____

_____

_____

_____

_____

_____

_____

_____

Author's Prayer

"Don't worry. God's got it!"

Dear heavenly Father,

Thank You for this precious opportunity to share what You have inspired me to write. May this book bless your people with the understanding of how to disable this intruding spirit and be ever encouraged to know You are always in the midst to bring us joy, peace, and happiness. I ask You, Lord, to continue to bless your people and protect them. May You shower your people with Your favor and give them Your peace. Amen.

"The end but not yours!"

(May a smile always be on your face and may the favor of God rest on your shoulders.)

Reverend Nadine Tyree Anderson
Author/Artist